SEEDS OF LOVE

A COUPLE'S DEVOTIONAL

—

KEMI AND BODE OLUTUNBI

SYNCTERFACE
Syncterface Media
London
www.syncterfacemedia.com

THIS
DEVOTIONAL

IS PRESENTED

To

_____

From

_____

SEEDS OF LOVE

(A COUPLE'S DEVOTIONAL)
52 WEEKLY DEVOTIONS TO GROW CLOSER TO GOD AND EACH OTHER

Copyright © 2022 Kemi and Bode Olutunbi

Cover design by Dami Odukoya Design

Published in the United Kingdom by Syncterface Media, London

This book is printed on acid-free paper

Foreword

Keeping God at the heart of your marriage is the key to having a successful and happy marriage. The word of God offers so much wisdom on how to build strong and healthy marriages. This devotional, Seeds of Love, draws on that wisdom, offering couples an opportunity to learn and grow in their love for God and for each other.

Filled with honest and heart-warming stories of Bode and Kemi's marriage journey, Godly principles and practical wisdom, it encourages the reader on their own journey. It is a useful resource for couples seeking to build strong and healthy marriages.

Look forward to a wonderful experience as you go through the pages.

~ Agu Irukwu ~

Senior Pastor
Jesus House for All the Nations

Preface

God's desire is that you have a beautiful and lasting marriage, where both husband and wife feel valued and appreciated and together fulfil God's purposes here on earth. Ecclesiastics 4:9-12 says that two are better than one because they have a good return for their labour. Praying together gives us access to God's power and helps us make daily choices that result in a fruitful lifelong marriage experience.

Our prayer is that Seeds of Love will give you an opportunity to share your heart with each other and grow in your love and understanding of each other and God and that Christ's presence will permeate every area of your marriage. Use this devotional to have conversations with your spouse and God each week and allow the Holy Spirit to fill you with the wisdom you need for a fulfilling and lasting marriage.

We would like to encourage you to keep track of what God is doing in you and with your marriage by using the companion Seeds of Love Couple's Journal.

Please also share your stories with us at seedsoflove@lovetalks.tv.

May God bless and preserve your marriage.

In His love and ours,
~ Kemi and Bode Olutunbi ~

@LOVETALKSTV
www.lovetalks.tv

Contents

Our Story

We met through a mutual friend and like many couples, we have two versions of our story, simply because we have different personalities and tend to see things differently from each other, a bit like a diagram of a block of cheese; depending on where you are looking at it from could look like a triangle, square or rectangle, different shapes but still the same block of cheese.

KEMI'S VERSION

I met Bode at my friend's house whilst I was on holiday in Nigeria, she had told me about a lovely Christian guy who would make the perfect husband for someone. Needless to say, Bode has no recollection of ever meeting me! Fast forward two years later, we finally meet when Bode relocated to the United Kingdom and my friend thought it was good for him to meet up with me. We both worked in the same industry and a little bit of help from me (Kemi) would enable him to settle down nicely into the UK, he said! At the time it never crossed my mind that I would get married to Bode, I simply regarded him as a good Christian brother so about six months down the line I was amazed when he told me God had told him I was his wife.

I was totally taken aback as never in my wildest imagination had I thought of him as a potential husband. However, with prayers good guidance and much more, we finally got married three years later and I realised God had given me a gift in him.

We were friends throughout the three years, we started dating in October, he proposed in February the following year and we were married later that year. It all seemed like a whirlwind and we have not looked back since. Our journey into married life began in earnest and I found out much later that my husband had prayed for me using Stormie Omartian's book; The Power of a Praying Husband, in the first few months of our marriage as he quickly realised that his expectations of marriage and his reality were very different.

BODE'S VERSION

Though slightly different, my recollection of how Kemi and I met and started our journey in marriage is essentially the same as hers. We met through a mutual friend who when I was relocating to the UK, mentioned that it would be helpful for me to get in touch with this really close friend of hers who lived in London and worked in the same sector as I had been working in Nigeria. This close friend was Kemi; who is now my wife.

I actually didn't get in touch with her for a while though, as I initially ended up in a city outside London and chose to return to the University there for further studies whilst adapting to life and work in the UK. I eventually made the call, heard the sweetest voicemail prompt ever, left the longest ever voicemail message possible, grew to develop a rather special friendship with her over the phone and eventually met up with her in London a few months later. Suffice to say that my sojourn outside London was doomed from that point on and it's safe to say that since then, we haven't looked back.

The grace of God has been abundant towards us. We eventually got engaged, got married and have stayed married through the years. Today, I'm truly grateful to God for using the friendship in Nigeria to bring me into the centre of His will for my life. He is faithful.

OUR STORY - A CONVERGENCE

One thing we are both in agreement about is that God has a great sense of humour, bringing us together as husband and wife with our different personalities, upbringing, backgrounds, outlook and dispositions and then calling us to serve others in their marriages. It has been and continues to be a profound mystery to us but a fulfilling and life-changing experience that is humbling. It continually reminds us of the vastness of the grace of God which calls out and brings out His riches that have been stored in us from eternity for His divine purposes.

Our journey in the marriage ministry began with attending the marriage course at Holy Trinity Church, Brompton as newlyweds; helping out as volunteers on the same course and subsequently setting up a marriage life group called "InSync" in our church, Jesus House, London. Eventually, we were asked by our Pastors to set up a Marriage ministry and Tightknots was birthed.

Like most couples, our marriage journey has been filled with ups and downs, but we are passionate about each other and the institution of marriage. We believe with every fibre of our being that Gods plan and desire is that every child of his has a great marriage that reflects His nature and leaves a legacy for generations to come.

How to Use the
Seeds of Love Devotional

In a world where we have so many demands on our time, it is important that we cultivate the habit of spending meaningful time together. Every marriage needs to be nurtured and spending time together in prayer is one way that you can strengthen your spiritual relationship together. An old saying states that a family that prays together stays together. Prayer is one of the most intimate things that a couple can do together. It gives us the opportunity to share our deepest feelings, thoughts and emotions with each other and with God and brings us to a deeper level of intimacy and compassion towards each other.

We have 52 weekly devotions linked to a scripture passage to help you as a married couple, understand God's blueprint for your marriage and give you practical insights into living this out daily. We recommend you allocate a time and a place that works for you both to read the devotional together, sharing your insights with the heart2heart, and ending with the prayers suggested and/or any other additional prayers that come to your mind. The personal reflection can be done individually and the Seeds of Love Couples Journal can be used as a tool to discuss and journal your journey as a couple.

Set aside the time to embark on this journey with each other. It might take between fifteen to thirty minutes each week. Time spent in the Word is powerful and will make a huge positive difference in your relationship.

Please do not forget to share your stories with us at seedsoflove@

lovetalks.tv. Join us on Twitter (**@Lovetalkstv**) and on Facebook and Instagram (**Lovetalkstv**).

LOYALTY FORGIVE PASSION
CONNECT INSPIRE
FUN
FORGIVE
OPENESS LOYALTY
CONNECT
O KINDNES
PASSION FUN
JOY LOVE
FORGIVE LOYALT

WEEK I

God's Design for Marriage

¹⁸ And the Lord God said, "It is not good that man should be alone; I will make him a helper comparable to him." ¹⁹Out of the ground the Lord God formed every beast of the field and every bird of the air, and brought them to Adam to see what he would call them. And whatever Adam called each living creature, that was its name. ²⁰So Adam gave names to all cattle, to the birds of the air, and to every beast of the field. But for Adam there was not found a helper comparable to him. ²¹And the Lord God caused a deep sleep to fall on Adam, and he slept; and He took one of his ribs, and closed up the flesh in its place. ²² Then the rib which the Lord God had taken from man He made into a woman, and He brought her to the man. ²³And Adam said: "This is now bone of my bones And flesh of my flesh; She shall be called Woman, Because she was taken out of Man." ²⁴Therefore a man shall leave his father and mother and be joined to his wife, and they shall become one flesh. ²⁵And they were both naked, the man and his wife, and were not ashamed.

~ Genesis 2:18-25 (NKJV)

God's creation at the beginning was perfected when He gave Eve to Adam. This was the first marriage and it signified the final act and completion of creation. Marriage is also used to illustrate the relationship between Christ and the Church, culminating in Jesus' return for His bride. Marriage is very important to God and He uses it to display His nature and person to the world.

God's desire is that we reflect Him in our marriages, mirroring the relationship between Christ and His bride with one another as husband and wife. People should look at our marriage and get a picture of who God is; a godly marriage is a powerful evangelistic tool as it showcases God's glory in a world where the regard in which marriage was once held has diminished greatly.

Adam was absolutely thrilled when he woke up to find Eve by his side and in the same manner, God expects us as His children to appreciate the gift that we are to each other. You can only get a benefit from what you receive and value, and more than ever, every spouse needs a partner who appreciates their value and regards them as a blessing simply by being part of their lives.

Heart2Heart

Does your marriage reflect the relationship between Christ and His bride? In what ways do you need to accept your spouse as God's gift to you? (Discuss)

Prayer

Pray that God's image will be reflected in your marriage and thank God for your spouse.

WEEK 2

Marriage - A Safe Haven

² Each one will be like a shelter from the wind and a refuge from the storm, like streams of water in the desert and the shadow of a great rock in a parched land.

~ Isaiah 32:2 (NIV)

As I (Bode) look back at our lives, I marvel at how frenetic life has been since we got married. We have experienced continuous competing demands on our family life and faced diverse life challenges including the loss of jobs, taking on the challenge of adult education, shouldering the mantle and demands of parenting, had the privilege of caring for our elderly parents, family bereavements, ...the list goes on. The strength we have received from God and each other to face these challenges together has made us realise more than ever that marriage is designed by God to be a safe haven from the storms and challenges of life.

We noticed early in our marriage that we each had a tendency to try and cope with demands and challenges by ourselves, so rather than running into each other's supporting arms, we ran away from each other and tried and cope with the demands and challenges by ourselves; I (Kemi) was fiercely independent and wanted to be seen as capable and I (Bode) wanted to shoulder the burdens by myself believing it was the man's role to shoulder burdens and be strong, not "weak".

When we run away from each other and shut out our spouses from our innermost thoughts, fears and insecurities, we miss the opportunity to draw closer to each other in order to experience true intimacy. Intimacy is built when we choose to be naked and unashamed; sharing our innermost thoughts, fears and insecurities without the fear of being judged or rejected. Intimacy is not only strengthened when we engage in the sexual act but every act of sharing is a move towards intimacy.

Our homes are designed by God to be places of rest where we come to get respite from the vagaries of life. Is your home a safe haven for you? For your spouse?

I (Kemi) remember a particularly difficult season of our lives when all that kept me going apart from God's grace was going home every day to Bode, who listened to me and prayed for me day after day during a particularly difficult season of caring for my mum who was ill.

Heart2Heart
How can your home be a safe haven? (Discuss)
Tell your spouse what you need from them to experience a safe haven marriage.

Prayer
Ask God to give you wisdom to build intimacy in your marriage and for every hindrance to intimacy to be removed in your marriage.

WEEK 3

A Vision for Your Marriage

² Then the LORD replied: "Write down the revelation and make it plain on tablets so that a herald may run with it.³ For the revelation awaits an appointed time; it speaks of the end and will not prove false. Though it linger, wait for it; it will certainly come and will not delay.

~ Habakkuk 2:2-3 (NIV)

Marriage is a partnership, and 'partnership' in the dictionary is defined as "A relationship between individuals or groups that is characterized by mutual cooperation and responsibility for the achievement of a specified goal".

God is a God of purpose bringing two people with different and complementary qualities together for their mutual benefit and to fulfil His purposes here on earth. Every couple needs to pray that God's purpose and plan for bringing them together will be fulfilled. God's vision for your marriage is to be discovered, as you pray God releases His dreams and desires into your heart for your marriage.

Heart2Heart
What dreams has God put into your heart for your marriage? How are you working as a team to fulfil God's vision for your marriage? (Discuss)

Prayer
Ask God to reveal His vision for your marriage and pray for the grace and wisdom to work as a team in fulfilling His vision.

Sex - A Divine Gift
(PART 1)

⁷ How beautiful are your sandaled feet, O queenly maiden. Your rounded thighs are like jewels, the work of a skilled craftsman. ² Your navel is perfectly formed like a goblet filled with mixed wine. Between your thighs lies a mound of wheat bordered with lilies. ³ Your breasts are like two fawns twin fawns of a gazelle. ⁴ Your neck is as beautiful as an ivory tower. Your eyes are like the sparkling pools in Heshbon by the gate of Bath-rabbim Your nose is as fine as the tower of Lebanon overlooking Damascus. ⁵ Your head is as majestic as Mount Carmel,and the sheen of your hair radiates royalty. The king is held captive by it stresses. ⁶ Oh, how beautiful you are! How pleasing, my love, how full of delights! ⁷ You are slender like a palm tree,and your breasts are like its clusters of fruit. ⁸ I said, "I will climb the palm tree and take hold of its fruit."May your breasts be like grape clusters, and the fragrance of your breath like apples. ⁹ May your kisses be as exciting as the best wine.

~ Song of Solomon 7:1-9 (NLT)

God designed our sex lives to be enjoyable and fulfilling. When God made a helpmate for Adam, she was suitable, complementary and adaptable to his needs – emotionally, physically and spiritually. When the first marriage was established, the joining of the male and the female entity into one would establish the covenant and set the stage for many more marriages. The physical affinity and spiritual connection Adam observed when first seeing Eve may have garnered his reaction of wonder-filled joy.

Sex is a very intimate act and God desires that we get to know our spouse even more intimately through the sexual act. Having the right attitude, a healthy view of sex, an understanding of our body and our spouse's body and responses are all important for an enjoyable sex life.

The sexual journey is one of discovery and there is a need for us to constantly discover each other. Adopting an attitude of due benevolence to each other ensures that each individual's needs are met and due benevolence is marked by kindness, sensitivity, love, charity, thoughtfulness, willingness without undue pressure and consideration.

A good sex life is not just confined to what happens in the bedroom, if you build your relationship outside of the bedroom, you will have a great sex life in the bedroom. Sex offers us a way of communicating our love for each other that no other means does. Enjoy your gift from God, invest in it and make time for it.

Heart2Heart
How can you make your sex life more fulfilling? (Discuss)

Prayer
Pray that you will always be attracted to each other.

Sex - A Divine Gift
(PART 2)

² But since sexual immorality is occurring, each man should have sexual relations with his own wife, and each woman with her own husband. ³ The husband should fulfill his marital duty to his wife, and likewise the wife to her husband. ⁴ The wife does not have authority over her own body but yields it to her husband. In the same way, the husband does not have authority over his own body but yields it to his wife. ⁵ Do not deprive each other except perhaps by mutual consent and for a time, so that you may devote yourselves to prayer. Then come together again so that Satan will not tempt you because of your lack of self-control.

~ 1 Corinthians 7:2-5 (NIV)

Sex involves the sealing of a covenant and the sexual act between husband and wife involves a physical, emotional and spiritual dimension. God designed sex for procreation and pleasure. He designed sex to be a fulfillment of the desires that He placed in us.

In the Bible the word "*know*" is used to refer to sexual inter- course and it is also the term used to describe our relationship with God. Sex is a spiritual activity and a form of worship and God's intention is that it is practiced in the confines of marriage to seal the marriage covenant.

Often times the reason some do not enjoy sex is because of guilt ridden feelings from past relationships, a distorted view of sex and inappropriate engagement of sex in the past, outside the confines of marriage. Our view of sex due to our backgrounds, family views, exposure and education, play a major role in our attitudes towards sex. Having a healthy view of sex is important. It is important that we adjust our attitudes to a biblical one.

Sex is a gift from God and with all good gifts, there is a purpose and use for the gift. A better understanding of the gift will result in an appropriate attitude and use of the gift.

A good sex life involves good communication between husband and wife in an atmosphere of openness, trust and vulnerability.

True sexual intimacy cannot be achieved by assumptions based on magazines, movies or internet images we have seen. As husbands and wives, we need to pray for each other and for ourselves that God will deliver us from any past encounters, as they distort God's design for sex between husband and wife.

Praying about our sex lives is also important as it will result in a more fulfilling sexual relationship with our spouse.

Heart2Heart
What is your attitude towards sex in your marriage? What might be holding you back from enjoying sex? (Discuss)

Prayer
Thank God for His gift of sex in your marriage? Are there any past hurts or fears that you may need to confess and pray for a release from together?

WEEK 6

The Gift of Oneness

²⁴ That is why a man leaves his father and mother and is united to his wife, and they become one flesh. ²⁵ Adam and his wife were both naked, and they felt no shame .

~ Genesis 2:24-25 (NIV)

Every decision you make in your marriage is either moving you towards each other or away from each other; our experiences, values and past affect our expectations of marriage. In order to enjoy the gift of oneness in your marriage, you need to adapt and make adjustments to accommodate your spouse. Rather than trying to change your spouse – an exercise in futility – focus on embracing the change that marriage brings to you and loving your spouse.

Experiencing challenges or difficulties in a marriage does not mean your marriage is doomed to failure, our responses to the challenges determine the outcome of our marriage.

Working through our issues together as a couple prevents us from retreating into our shells or blaming and attacking each other. Embracing oneness is working together against the external forces threatening our marriage.

Dennis Rainey in his book, "Staying Close" says that "Oneness in marriage involves complete unity with each other. It's more than a mere mingling of two humans – It's a tender merger of body, soul and spirit"

Heart2Heart
In what ways are you embracing the gift of oneness in your marriage?
Are there areas where you are moving away from each other? What
changes can you make now to stop this drift? (Discuss)

Prayer
Ask God for wisdom to make the right choices and decisions that
will engender oneness.

Loving Your Wife

⁷ In the same way, you husbands must give honour to your wives. Treat your wife with understanding as you live together. She may be weaker than you are, but she is your equal partner in God's gift of new life. Treat her as you should so your prayers will not be hindered.

~ 1Peter 3:7 (NLT)

The scripture above encourages us husbands to honour our wives and treat them with understanding so that our prayers will not be hindered. As I reflect on this, I (Bode) think about countless times when it has seemed to me that women are a lot more complex than men are.

When I think of my wife and my interactions with her sometimes, especially when her words and actions are in conflict, and when what she says is not actually what she means, it can be quite challenging trying to understand her, yet I am required by God to dwell with her in understanding despite her "complexities".

I marvel at how "spot on" God's word as quoted above is regarding the need to treat her with understanding.

It is far easier said than done at these times. In fact, the easier road to follow is to come to the conclusion that my wife is too complicated; she has a problem and when she is ready to change, I will relate properly with her. The danger with this approach is that it is dishonouring to her and does not honour Christ's command to love her persistently, sacrificially and unendingly.

During these times, God will often remind me to appreciate the value that she is bringing to our marriage, her contribution to our diversity, her sensitive and intuitive nature.

I can be so logical and focused on the goal that I sometimes miss the experience and opportunities that could be shared during the journey, the little insinuations, thoughtfulness, unsaid or unwritten things that make such a big difference and add some spice to our relationship.

Every attempt at understanding and pleasing your wife is honouring to God, there is also a joy that comes from knowing that you are making your wife happy when you see the genuine smile or expression of appreciation on her face. Loving your wife in the way that God desires, enables her to become who God has called her to be. A love that is sacrificial puts her needs before yours and makes her believe the best of herself.

Every wife needs a husband who believes in her, loving her means listening to her and taking an interest in things that pertain to her needs. Over the years one of the ways that I (Bode) have realised communicates my love for Kemi is taking a keen interest in her and the things she likes. I recall a few years ago when she wanted to go swimming regularly, I decided to go with her not because I particularly like swimming but because I wanted to encourage her and express my interest in her and support for her. This simple decision and investment in our relationship has paid dividends to me in many ways even though my intention was to give my time and attention to her.

Heart2Heart

Ask your wife what loving her means to her, in what ways can you show love to her this week? ("The five love languages" is an excellent book by Gary Chapman and describes the five ways that people want to beloved). (Discuss)

Prayer
Ask God to open your eyes to the things that communicate love to your wife.

WEEK 8

Honouring Your Husband

¹ Wives, in the same way submit yourselves to your own husbands so that, if any of them do not believe the word, they may be won over without words by the behaviour of their wives, ² when they see the purity and reverence of your lives.

~ 1 Peter 3:1-2 (NIV)

As I (Kemi) think about the scripture above that encourages us to be submissive wives, I am reminded of "Ezer", the original Hebrew word used to describe a wife's role as a helper. This word is also used to refer to God as our helper. This suggests to me that as a helper I have what my husband needs. Being a submissive wife does not in any way suggest that as wives we are of lesser value than our husbands, rather it means coming alongside our husbands and taking our rightful place in God's order. Wives will agree that it is a lot easier to submit when you know that your husband has your best interest at heart. We are asked to submit to our husband out of obedience to God and not as a result of our husband's conduct. Our husband's conduct cannot be a prerequisite for our submission. Submission is not conditional or dependent on our husband's action. Please note though, that this does not apply to being party to a husband's sinful or abusive behaviour. God is a kind and loving father who has our best interest at heart. If he is asking us to be submissive wives, it is for our benefit.

Every husband needs a wife who is a cheerleader, who appreciates and respects him. Respecting him means noticing him (paying him attention), valuing him, admiring him, cherishing him. It seems a tall order, but if God is asking us to do it, by His grace we can. It is an intentional act of focusing on what is good about our husband rather than his weaknesses.

Remember; what you focus on gets magnified. One of the ways that I (Kemi) communicate respect to Bode is minding how I speak to him, ensuring that my words are respectful and listening to him. There are times when he wants to share his thoughts, plans and dreams with me, and I so badly want to give my opinions and ask questions on how exactly these plans are going to work What he needs when he is sharing a dream is for me to listen, dream with him and come along to offer my help. Asking him questions when he is sharing will feel to him like criticism of what is still just a seed in his heart. These questions are important, but only in their proper time. I am learning to exercise restraint and not kill a dream before it is birthed. I get it wrong sometimes, but the more I offer my listening ears, the more he shares his dreams with me in a safe environment.

The test of our submission includes situations when the house has been left in a state, when the kitchen sink is full and I have just come back from a hard day's work, when he seems to want to spend more time at the office or out with his friends than at home... These situations are when the rubber hits the road and respecting and honouring our husbands simply because God commanded it kicks in.

Learning to know what to say and when, for my husband to feel respected is an ongoing battle, yet persevering will yield results in becoming the custodian of his heart and dreams.

Heart2Heart
Ask your husband what respect means to him. When does he feel respected (by you or by others)? When does he feel disrespected? (Discuss)
List two things you can stop or start doing now to show respect to your husband.

22

Prayer
Ask God for insight into meeting your husband's need for respect.

A Mutual Responsibility to Love

FOR MEN

²¹ Submit to one another out of reverence for Christ.
²⁵ Husbands, love your wives, just as Christ loved the church and gave himself up for her ²⁶ to make her holy, cleansing[a]her by the washing with water through the word, ²⁷ and to present her to himself as a radiant church, without stain or wrinkle or any other blemish, but holy and blameless. ²⁸ In this same way, husbands ought to love their wives as their own bodies. He who loves his wife loves himself. ²⁹ After all, no one ever hated their own body, but they feed and care for their body, just as Christ does the church.

~ Ephesians 5:21,25-29 (NIV)

In marriage, both husband and wife are called to love and submit to each other out of reverence for Christ (Ephesians 5:22). Agape love, which is the highest love, can only work when both parties are in submission to one another. Submission means laying down your independent will for each other.

Husbands are to love their wives as Christ loved the Church, Christ's love is marked by giving, a sacrificial type of love, giving of Himself by yielding and exchanging a lofty position for a lower position (Philippians 2:8 tells us he 'humbled himself') to better understand and appropriate his love for the Church. He used his authority and power to make the Church special; His words cleansed her, gave her vision and hope. In the same vein, a husband is required to provide the right environment for his wife to flourish through sacrificial/ servant leadership.

Praying and sharing your vision with your wife will help build trust in your marriage – and will show that she matters. Involving her in the vision will go a long way in reassuring her of your love. A wise husband values his wife as a helper and sacrificially loves his wife. Loving your wife needs to be communicated not only in words but also with consistent, appropriate and convincing actions.

Heart2Heart
Is the love you are showing to your wife reflecting the love Christ shows the Church? In what ways can you show sacrificial leadership to your wife? (Discuss)

Prayer
Thank God for your wife and ask for grace to lead her and your family as Christ leads the Church.

A Mutual Responsibility to Love

FOR WOMEN

21 Submit to one another out of reverence for Christ.
25 Husbands, love your wives, just as Christ loved the church and gave himself up for her 26 to make her holy, cleansing[a]her by the washing with water through the word, 27 and to present her to himself as a radiant church, without stain or wrinkle or any other blemish, but holy and blameless. 28 In this same way, husbands ought to love their wives as their own bodies. He who loves his wife loves himself. 29 After all, no one ever hated their own body, but they feed and care for their body, just as Christ does the church.

~ Ephesians 5:21,25-29 (NIV)

In marriage, both husband and wife are called to love and submit to each other out of reverence for Christ (Ephesians 5:22). Agape love, which is the highest love can only work when both parties are in submission to one another. Submission means laying down your independent will for each other.

Wives are admonished to submit to their husband's leadership in the home by understanding and supporting their husbands in ways that honour the Master. Submission requires the wife to love her husband and should not be seen as an excuse to take the back seat or be complacent or be a doormat, but rather as an opportunity to "fit" into God's prescribed order for marriage.

This order, if practised properly, would create an environment where the husband's headship and leadership can be maximised to achieve mutual benefit and God's divine purpose.

A wife should help incubate and support her husband's vision/ plans. Both the husband and wife's God-given vision are meant to work together to fulfil His plans for their lives.

Submission should be unconditional, evident in trusting his decisions and judgments, whilst constantly praying for him. One of a man's primary needs is to be respected. He also desires admiration and praise. Submission engenders an environment where the husband can receive these gifts.

Heart2Heart
Are you submitting to your husband as unto the Lord? In what ways can you show submission to your husband? (Discuss)

Prayer
Thank God for your husband and ask for grace to submit to him as Christ modelled submission to the father.

God's Plans For Your Marriage

¹¹ For I know the plans I have for you," declares the Lord, "plans to prosper you and not to harm you, plans to give you hope and a future.

~ Jeremiah 29:11 (NIV)

At the Jesus House Couples' Weekend Away in 2005 we heard a talk titled; "And It Was Good". The talk was based on the biblical text on God's creation of the world and at the end of each verse after God created something, the phrase "and God saw that it was good" was used. It was definitely a eureka moment for me in that it put a greater desire and longing in my heart to experience the "*good*" that God meant when he created the concept of marriage.

God has a plan and desire for your marriage, and finding out and living out His will for your marriage will make your marriage a successful one. A good marriage is not defined by other people's standards or your standards but by God's standard.

Regardless of where you are in experiencing the "good" that God has for you, it is important to keep checking in with God and asking for His help in fulfilling His plans for you as a couple. There is a purpose for every marriage – yes, including yours! Why don't you ask God what His purpose is for you in this season?

Heart2Heart
Do you know what God's plans for your marriage are? Discuss what you have heard him saying in the past or to you as individuals recently. (Discuss)

Prayer
Ask Him to reveal His plans for your marriage and pour out His grace for you to be willing and obedient.

Pillars of a Successful Marriage
CLEAVING

[24] Therefore shall a man leave his father and his mother, and shall cleave unto his wife: and they shall be one flesh.

~ Genesis 2:24 (KJV)

'Cleave' is an old-fashioned word meaning 'to stick fast or adhere': imagine two sheets of paper glued together, when you pick it up, it's no longer two sheets, but one, with two sides.

Cleaving to your spouse is about allowing your marriage relationship to take priority over all other relationships so that you are free to establish a new family unit that is independent of your parents. It is only possible to truly cleave to your spouse when your marriage takes priority over all other relationships.

A marriage presents a change in the dynamics of existing relationships with family and friends. Where this change is not handled properly it can adversely affect the marriage relationship. It is important that each spouse acknowledges and recognises this change and makes a conscious decision to redefine their existing relationships to reflect the fact that they are now a couple. For example, letting your extended family know that you need to discuss things, including potential plans, with your spouse before committing to them. Another way to cleave is to involve your spouse in your decision making as it relates to your extended family.

It is always a great help when parents help and accept the "*new order*" when their children get married by giving them much needed space to adjust to the "new order" and do not make unnecessary demands that seek to test the "new order". Where parents do not respect the boundaries, it can be very challenging for the parties concerned. Honouring our parents is important and firmly maintaining the boundaries by showing love while remaining firm and united in our responses as a couple towards them goes a long way in helping everyone adjust to the "new order".

It requires re-arranging priorities so as to reflect the changes that marriage brings and it takes time to get used to but once the attitude is geared towards this ideal, then everything will gradually fall into place. Leaving to cleave does not mean severing all other relationships but it means working together on all our relationships as one team.

Whether you are newly married or not, it is very important to talk about how you manage other relationships. Other relationships should always complement and not compete with our love.

Heart2Heart
How are you and your spouse doing in cleaving to each other and managing other relationships? (Discuss)

Prayer
Ask God to help you and your spouse cleave to one another, and to help you navigate the transition with care and sensitivity all round.

Pillars of a Successful Marriage

ONENESS

[24] Therefore shall a man leave his father and his mother, and shall cleave unto his wife: and they shall be one flesh.

~ Genesis 2:24 (KJV)

Marriage is a journey, not a destination and the ultimate goal of marriage is for the two to become one. The Greek word for marriage is **gameo** (meaning to fuse together).

Oneness should permeate every aspect of a married couple's existence. For example, take two sets of liquids, oil and water and water and blackcurrant squash. Mix each pair together and observe what happens. Which one do you think represents God's goal for oneness in marriage?

There shouldn't be any uncharted territory i.e., 'no-go' areas, in your marriage, from your sexual union to your finances; the goal should be geared towards walking in oneness, unified in body (sexual union), soul (mind and will) and spirit (belief). However, the journey of oneness is a lifelong one that requires deliberate effort on each person's part and a brokenness and willingness to change.

For each couple to move towards integration there needs to be one vision, however, due to differing perspectives, effective communication is essential to actualising the vision of oneness. The recognition of your spouse as integral to the successful fulfilment of your destiny is a necessary first step in this process of integration. The Bible records Adam's cry of recognition when he saw his partner: "This is now bone of my bones and flesh of my flesh". Nobody can be more closely related to you than your spouse.

Heart2Heart
Are you one with each other? Identify things that need to change in your relationship for oneness to thrive. (Discuss)

Prayer
Ask God to reveal hindrances to you and your spouse becoming one.

Pillars of a Successful Marriage

NAKED AND UNASHAMED

[24] That is why a man leaves his father and mother and is united to his wife, and they become one flesh. Adam and his wife were both naked, and they felt no shame.

~ Genesis 2:24 (KJV)

The foundation laid at the start of a marriage is very important. A foundation of openness and honesty from the beginning will help towards building intimacy. Revealing our true and deepest feelings to our spouses, helps us know each other. When we are vulnerable with each other, communicating truthfully with each other, we build trust and invoke God's protection on our relationship. This helps us to truly become one.

We can create a safe atmosphere for our spouse that allows them to be vulnerable by respecting them and accepting their weaknesses. Nobody is perfect and we all have areas in our lives that we would rather not share with other people.

It is important that when we are vulnerable, by sharing intimately with our spouse, the information shared is never used as a weapon to pull each other down but as a tool to build intimacy in the relationship.

Heart2Heart

Are there areas where you need to apologise to each other for using the other's vulnerability against them? Are there areas you are afraid

34

to disclose to each other? Discuss how you can move towards being emotionally 'naked and unashamed' with each other.

Prayer
Ask God to help you to trust one another and be trustworthy partners, so you can grow to be naked and unashamed with each other.

Pillars of a Successful Marriage

INTIMACY (PART 1)

> ²⁵ *Adam and his wife were both naked, and they felt no shame*
>
> ~ Genesis 2:25 (NIV)

Marriage counsellors cite a lack of communication as one of the leading causes of marital breakdown. Good communication in a marriage can be likened to what blood is to life; without good communication in a marriage, the relationship is non-existent.

Every spouse needs to learn the art of communication. Effective communication is ensuring that the following five components mean the same thing to both parties; **(1)** What you meant to say **(2)** What you actually said **(3)** How you said it **(4)** What I thought you said and **(5)** What I heard you say. The trick is ensuring that all five are conveying the same message.

It involves listening to your spouse with your heart and eyes, with the intention of seeking to understand them more. True communication is a skill. It must be deliberate and requires learning. It does not happen naturally, and choosing the right timing is everything.

I (Bode) remember the early days of our marriage when I was a serial interrupter and Kemi was a reluctant communicator, communication – especially discussing difficult issues – seemed like pulling out a tooth without any anaesthetics. Thankfully, applying some of the skills we have learnt over the years has improved our communication greatly. As a serial interrupter, I often spoke without giving the opportunity for Kemi a reluctant communicator, to share her thoughts. I had to learn to tease out information from Kemi by asking her open-ended questions such as, "What do you think?", "Why might you be feeling this way?" etc whilst allowing and giving her the opportunity to think through her feelings and thoughts without trying to force my way into her thoughts.

I (Kemi) also needed to learn to express my feelings and thoughts to Bode knowing that he was a safe place and I could trust him. I (Kemi) have also learnt to communicate and share my feelings and thoughts so that Bode can better understand me rather than before when I would be quiet and not say anything other than "I am processing my thoughts and will get back to you" which Bode found very frustrating in the earlier years of marriage.

As the times have gone on I (Bode) have learnt that drawing out a reluctant communicator through open-ended questions has helped to ensure that we hear each other better. Choosing the right moments to talk and share from our hearts has been helpful.

Trying to talk when one of us is tired or hungry or watching a favourite TV programme will not result in a good outcome. Most importantly offering a safe and accepting environment for our spouse to share is a good communication enhancer.

Heart2Heart
How can you communicate better with each other? What bad communication habits do you need to change individually and as a couple? (Discuss)

Prayer
Ask God to pour out His grace upon you and your spouse to be able to communicate effectively and lovingly.

Pillars of a Successful Marriage

INTIMACY (PART 2)

> *²⁵ Adam and his wife were both naked, and they felt no shame*
>
> ~ Genesis 2:25 (NIV)

We live in a highly sexualised culture which makes intimacy challenging, we are constantly surrounded and bombarded with images suggesting we be perfect, and by films promoting passion but rarely intimacy. This can make being vulnerable with each other challenging as it takes courage to go against the grain of the "perfection" culture yet the scripture above depicts a picture of a husband and wife who were unashamed. They were unashamed, as sin had not entered into the world; however, the minute they sinned they wanted to cover their nakedness. Our desire to hide ourselves from each other is a result of the sinful nature in us. However, God's redemption of us through Christ offers an opportunity for us to find freedom, love and acceptance with each other as husband and wife in a godly marriage.

Marriage gives us an up-close and personal view of our spouse; the good, the bad and the ugly. Yet, God offers us an opportunity to show His love to our spouse through our acceptance of our spouse, loving our spouse despite their imperfections. Living out a godly marriage where there is no fear of rejection breeds love and commitment.

Marriage presents us with the opportunity to show the Christ kind of love to our spouse on a daily basis with God continually supplying His grace to love our spouse.

Building intimacy is like moving from the shallow end of the pool to the deep end, moving from trivial talk to sharing our innermost and deepest thoughts without the fear of rejection in an environment of vulnerability, transparency, openness and honesty.

A marriage where a couple are naked and unashamed is a beauty to behold and one to be experienced rather than described as it brings honour to God

Heart2Heart
In what ways can you increase intimacy in your marriage? (Discuss)

Prayer
Pray that God will help you to build intimacy with each other.

Pillars of a Successful Marriage

INTIMACY (PART 3)

²⁵ Adam and his wife were both naked, and they felt no shame

~ Genesis 2:25 (NIV)

Communication is the lifeline of a marriage. Without good communication the marriage relationship is non-existent. In his book, "The Triangle of Love", John Sterberg identified three essential components of love in a marriage: Passion, Intimacy and Commitment.

Commitment is the decision to love and stay together. Passion is the physical attraction or strong desire to be with each other sexually. Intimacy is mutual disclosure, affection, validation, support, and the desire to share things. He says you can think of 'intimacy' as meaning, "Into-me-see".

It is only through effective communication that we can develop intimacy in a marriage. Communication is often seen as merely conversing; however, it is much more than that. a complex exchange of thoughts (ideas, opinions, plans, judgment), knowledge (facts, information) and feelings (emotions).

Effective communication occurs only in an environment where both individuals have the liberty to be vulnerable enough to express their true feelings, thoughts or knowledge, through listening, watching/observing and sharing/talking.

Heart2Heart
Does your spouse feel free to communicate freely with you? If not, what are the barriers to your communication?

What steps do you need to take to foster an environment where communication is safe and mutually vulnerable? (Discuss)

Prayer
Ask God to help you build genuine intimacy in your marriage.

Pillars of a Successful Marriage

LISTENING: THE WAY TO YOUR WIFE'S HEART

19 My dear brothers and sisters, take note of this: Everyone should be quick to listen

~ James 1:19 (NIV)

Listening to each other is a wonderful gift that you can give to each other. Whilst buying a present or planning a surprise for each other are all good in themselves, listening to your spouse makes them feel valued and special.

It is about giving each other time and undivided attention, helping each other feel secure in your love. When I (Kemi) think of fond memories in our marriage they are marked by times that Bode listened to me and showed that what mattered to me mattered to him – especially as he had to exercise great restrain not to give me solutions! I (Bode) can attest to the fact men are wired differently from women, when we are engaging in conversations, we are usually thinking of offering solutions to the matters raised in a conversation, this might come as a surprise to our wives who just want us to listen to them without offering solutions.

The goal from a wife's perspective is to feel heard and listened to. Every husband needs to learn to be a good listener. Time spent listening to your wife is not the best time to give a solution to what she is sharing with you, except she expressly asks you for one. For a woman, sharing a problem is paramount whilst for a man, solving a problem is paramount.

When you are having a good conversation with your spouse, you are both giving each other your undivided attention. It helps you to feel connected to each other, learn more about each other and gain a better understanding of each other.

It is often said that every wife wants her husband to listen to her and that a great husband is one who has learnt to listen to his wife with his ears, eyes and heart. We have certainly found that to be true in our marriage.

Heart2Heart
How can you learn to listen to your wife? Ask her to share with you the things that you do that make her feel special and listened to. (Discuss)

Prayer
Ask God to help you listen to your wife and enjoy spending time with her.

Pillars of a Successful Marriage

RESPECT: THE WAY TO YOUR HUSBAND'S HEART

² *When they observe the pure and modest way in which you conduct yourselves, together with your reverence [for your husband. That is, you are to feel for him all that reverence includes] - to respect, defer to, revere him; [revere means] to honour, esteem (appreciate, prize), and [in the human sense] adore him; [and adore means] to admire, praise, be devoted to, deeply love and enjoy [your husband*

~ 1 Peter 3:2 (AMPC)

Husbands usually say that it is not what their wives said that made them angry, it was the way that it was said that they found disrespectful. As wives, our words matter to our husbands. According to Dr. Emerson Eggerichs, the author of Love and Respect, the way a woman speaks to her husband is important as her words and tone can push her husband to silence and make him feel rejected.

It is always helpful when having conversations with your husband, to begin with the end in mind, thinking of the outcome you want from the conversation and tailoring your speech to achieve that result. For example, if I (Kemi) want to ask for Bode's help, applying this principle would look like this; Bode, please it would be helpful if you could put the children to bed at night on Monday and Tuesday as it would give me some time to prepare for some important work meetings, I have coming up this week.

A not so helpful way of conveying the same idea would look like this; "Bode, I think it is only proper that you help out with putting the children to bed on Monday and Tuesday night. You never help with the children and besides I have some crucial meetings coming up this week and I need to prepare."

Knowing that respect is important to a man means that we must carefully consider and weigh our words. What a wife says to her husband matters a lot to him.

Heart2Heart
Are your words or tone of voice showing respect to your husband? What do you need to stop doing? What do you need to start doing? (Discuss)

Prayer
Pray for wisdom to be able to communicate with your husband in a way that shows respect for him.

Loving Against All Odds

2 Not looking to your own interests but each of you to the interests of the others.

~ Philippians 2:4 (NIV)

As I (Bode) sit down to reflect on the marriage covenant, I realise that a lot of our culture today is based on a "my rights" principle; equity and equality are the name of the game. Whilst I appreciate that this is the way that order is maintained in society, I cannot help but think that a marriage relationship that is based on each partner doing their bit, a 50/50 mentality, is doomed to fail. A marriage where one's acceptance of one's partner is based on their performance is destined for failure.

Life is filled with situations and circumstances that we did not anticipate or bargain for. When we take our marriage vows, we do not know what the future holds. If we have not settled in our hearts that our love is till death do us part, when those situations arise, we are likely to be disappointed and to respond in ways that put our marriage in jeopardy. How do you account for the loss of income when a spouse loses their job if the marriage relationship is based on a 50/50 mentality? What happens when a spouse cannot meet their end of the bargain because of ill health, an accident etc. There are so many situations that show that marriage is meant to be based on unconditional love, where acceptance is not based on performance and giving of yourself to your spouse is not based on their performance.

Challenges have a way of either driving us apart or close without God's perspective in our marriage we are likely to think and respond in a manner that inevitably leads to failure. How do you keep account of who is doing more than the other?

Remember that our marriage vows are sacred, promising to love each other for better, for worse, for richer, for poorer, in sickness and in health, till death us do part, according to God's holy law. Marriage is a covenant and a covenant is initiated for the benefit of the other person (other-centred not self-centred), it is about us seeking to give rather than what we can receive.

Heart2Heart
How can you build your friendship (**phileo**) love in your marriage? In what ways have you begun to accept a 50/50 mentality in your marriage and what can you do to change this? (Discuss)

Prayer
Ask God for forgiveness and grace to live out your marriage vows and to build your friendship.

Your Number One Priority

¹³ Greater love has no one than this: to lay down one's life for one's friends.
~ John 15:13 (NIV)

Find ways every day to let your spouse know they are number one in your life, next to the Lord, of course. Be unreservedly their greatest fan. Find out what is most important to your spouse and spare no expense in money (within reason of course) and effort to ensure your spouse has it. If it is your affirmation; shower it on your spouse. If it is your support do not deny your spouse. If it is your texts and emails, schedule them into your day. Get creative, find 365 ways of showing your love throughout this year. Basically, celebrate your spouse, let them know you truly appreciate and value them. Do not just lend a hand, give your heart!

Love is self-sacrificing. Take a vacation from the telly if need be! On a serious note, television is certainly a poor substitute for real life. We spend a huge chunk of the best parts of our day with others at work and elsewhere. It is heart-rending when the TV habit takes away the few hours that are left for your spouse and children.

Choose to have regular times that are set aside exclusively for your spouse and make the extra effort to engage with each other on a deeper level. Of course, it goes without saying that if your wife wants a back rub on the afternoon of the FA Cup final, there is no better time to show her how much you really care!

Although I must add that these may not be the best times for wives to ask for a back rub. Laying down our lives for each other is sometimes hard; it means going out of one's way for your spouse and putting your plans and pleasures aside.

Heart2Heart

Does your spouse know they are your number one priority? If not why not tell them? Even if they already know, a gentle reminder will not hurt. Words only go so far, though - talk about what little things you can do this week to demonstrate you mean it. (Discuss)

Prayer

Lord, help me to lay down my own life willingly for my spouse, to show them they are my priority.

Protecting Your Marriage

AFFAIR PROOF YOUR MARRIAGE

8 Whoever digs a pit may fall into it; whoever breaks through a wall may be bitten by a snake

~ Ecclesiastes 10:8 (NIV)

It is important to protect your marriage. In the course of our daily lives we will encounter attractive people of the opposite sex and it is vital that we do not give in to temptation. Research shows that at least 60% of people who end up having extramarital affairs did not plan to, it all started in an innocuous way until they found themselves on a slippery slope that ended disastrously.

The devil offers extramarital affairs as a means of escaping from the truth, giving the notion that the grass is greener on the other side, whilst setting people up for untold pain, misery and destruction with dire consequences.

Extramarital affairs can come in many shapes, not just with the opposite sex. Anything that takes precedence over our spouse and that we lend our affections to can so easily become an extramarital affair e.g., married to the job, sports, materialism, pornography etc.

We hear so many stories of extramarital affairs we are told began with an innocent comment to a spouse at a vulnerable period, a work colleague noticing their appearance, a friend giving an ignored spouse a listening ear etc. Paying attention to each other as well as cultivating and tending your marriage is important so that the enemy does not get a foothold.

Heart2Heart
What can you do to affair-proof your marriage? (Discuss)

Prayer
Ask God to protect your marriage and help you stay faithful to your vows.

Protecting Your Marriage

LET GO OF PAST RELATIONSHIPS

15 Catch all the foxes, those little foxes, before they ruin the vineyard of love, for the grapevines are blossoming
~ Song of Solomon 2:15 (NLT)

A few years ago, when we were getting ready to move from our flat and having a clear-out, we found a box that had pictures in it, including pictures and letters from previous relationships. We had a good discussion and both agreed that it was best that we got rid of them. It might seem to some to be an extreme measure – after all, we had been married for a while and were completely besotted with each other. But we were aware that temptations do not always come in ways that we would recognise them. A little reminiscing about an ex, secret longings from the past, trips down memory lane could easily begin to very subtly chip away at our love for each other.

When was the last time you heard from an ex? Have you been checking out your ex on Facebook and other social media? Do you have a box of letters or cards from previous relationships? Marriage is about the two of you excluding all others, we are called to help dispel our spouse's insecurities and build them up. If your spouse is expressing concerns about a previous relationship you had, do not ignore their concerns; the enemy is a good deceiver and he comes to steal, kill and destroy, do not allow the 'foxes' to ruin your vineyard of love.

Heart2Heart

Do you still think about an old flame? Be honest with yourself and with your spouse. Ask their forgiveness and work out together what steps you will take to ensure that neither of you is open to this kind of temptation. (Discuss)

Prayer

Ask God to help you forsake all others and cling to your spouse alone.

Protecting Your Marriage

LAY ASIDE THE WEIGHT

¹ Therefore, since we are surrounded by such a great cloud of witnesses, let us throw off everything that hinders and the sin that so easily entangles. And let us run with perseverance the race marked out for us
~ Hebrews 12:1 (NIV)

As someone who has battled with losing weight, I (Kemi) know how uncomfortable carrying extra weight can be. Our marriage needs to be free of weights so that we can enjoy the blessings that God has prepared for us and enjoy a satisfying and fulfilling experience.

These weights could be things like our fears and failures, things that have hurt us, or negative mindsets that are not aligned to God's word and can have a deep hold on shaping who we are and how we relate to the world and other people. We need to let go of these things so that we are able to give of ourselves fully to our marriage. We might need some professional Christian counselling or pastoral care to help us work through these issues and we should not hesitate to get such help.

Sometimes our experiences from past relationships can hinder and affect our marriage relationship. Getting rid of the weights involves having an honest introspection, thinking carefully about pain and hurt from the past and inviting the Holy Spirit into your heart to heal you totally so that you can quit blaming others and hiding your real self from your spouse.

Heart2Heart
Ask God to reveal any weights from the past that may be hindering your marriage. (Discuss)

Prayer
Pray for God's strength to let go and be free in the liberty that Christ has already purchased for you.

Protecting Your Marriage

GUARD YOUR HEART

23 Above all else guard your heart for it is the wellspring of life
~ Proverbs 4:23 (NIV)

There are so many temptations coming into our homes these days. From the TV programmes that celebrate sexual immorality to the websites that lure people into pornography, the onslaught of the enemy is unprecedented. In the past, to access these, you had to go outside to bring them into your home; now they are easily accessible right inside our homes. Unless you make the choices to prevent them from invading your home they will remain as uninvited, unwelcome, but very real guests.

The enemy's intent with the temptations is to lure us into seeing our spouses and marriages differently causing a distortion, using pictures and images with subliminal messages that are driven by the spirits of lust and self. His sole aim is to create a wedge between spouses, creating unreasonable expectations for your spouse and marriage.

It is important that we guard the 'gates' of our minds – our eyes and ears – as what we see and hear will have an impact on what we think about our spouses.

Heart2Heart

In what way do you need to guard your heart and protect your marriage? What programmes do you need to stop watching? Do you have sufficient pornography filters and blockers set up on all Internet-enabled devices you have access to? (Discuss)

Prayer
Ask God for power to overcome temptation and to make wise decisions in what you allow in your home.

Choose Life

Every day in our marriages we are confronted with choices and decisions that we need to take; these are opportunities that we are presented with to make a choice for God and turn away from sin.

Every right choice we make with regards to our marriage, our treatment of our spouse and our responses to our spouse is a victory for the kingdom of God and a blow to the kingdom of darkness, storing up rewards in eternity where it really matters.

When we give in to temptation, we give the enemy an opportunity to attack our relationship; obedience to God ensures that we live victoriously.

I (Kemi) remember the early days of marriage when I struggled with the necessary adjustments required to adapt to married life. Prior to being married, I was used to my company, doing things my own way and suddenly I was faced with a new life, living with Bode, sharing "my space" with someone who wanted to talk when I wanted to be quiet and just be. At these times, I would refuse to talk and say things like I just want to be left alone and not respond. I (Bode) on the other hand was bewildered by such responses as I longed to talk to my wife and share our "space". I (Kemi) used to marvel at how Bode would still be kind towards me, making me a cup of tea whilst making his and not respond to my sulking.

Whilst I did not tell him at the time, his behaviour challenged me and often convicted me of my lack of "Christ-likeness" in dealing with him. I wonder where we would be today if he had reacted in the same way towards me. Every opportunity you get to model Christ to your spouse in your conduct is worth it.

Think about your choice today and choose life.

Heart2Heart
What temptations do you need to overcome in your marriage? (Discuss)

Prayer
Pray for help and grace to overcome temptation and be victorious.

Marriage Robber

STRIFE

¹⁰ The thief comes only to steal and kill and destroy; I have come that they may have life, and have it to the full

~ John 10:10 (NIV)

Conflict is inevitable in marriage because of our different temperaments and dispositions. Our differences inform our expectations and when these expectations are not met, a conflict develops.

Conflict occurs when our desires are not fulfilled or our expectations are not met; when we do not get what we want or we feel our rights have been violated. We feel hurt, and this can lead to fighting and quarrelling.

We need to be aware that fighting and quarrelling can lead to strife. Strife gives the enemy an opportunity to steal, kill and destroy in a home. Conflict does not have to lead to strife – constructive conflict is good and actually provides opportunities for building intimacy and growth in the marriage. It is our response to conflict that causes strife, and our response is our responsibility. Always remember your spouse is not your enemy – you are on the same side!

Heart2Heart
How do you resolve conflict? Is it healthy? (Discuss)

Prayer
Ask God for wisdom to handle and deal with conflict in a healthy manner.

Marriage Robber

SELFISHNESS

³ Do nothing out of selfish ambition or vain conceit. Rather, in humility value others above yourselves, ⁴ not looking to your own interests but each of you to the interests of the others

~ Philippians 2:3-4 (NIV)

Each person has a natural inclination to be self-centred and the prevailing culture is very much focused on self and tolerant of selfishness. However, marriage God's way is not about me but about having an "us" mentality. The secret to a great marriage is putting your spouse's needs before yours. What happens when what you consider priority and a need for you is not what your spouse thinks? Whose decision would overrule the *priority vs needs* response? Conflict most often comes when what I want comes into conflict with what my spouse wants. My selfishness rears its head and I dig in my heels, not wanting to surrender my will.

Selfishness focuses on what I can get from my spouse and how they can meet my needs, whilst selflessness focuses on what I can give and how I can meet my spouse's needs.

Making a choice to prefer our spouse brings glory to God as we honour him by our obedience. Jesus' relationship with the Church, His bride, illustrates the kind of self-giving, sacrificial, serving love that he calls us to live out towards our spouse.

A selfless and successful marriage is made up of two people preferring each other and seeking to meet each other's needs rather than seeking to have their needs met.

Heart2Heart
In what ways have you been selfish in your marriage? What can you do to make amends? (Discuss)

Prayer
Ask God to help you model the Christ kind of love to your spouse, putting your spouse first.

Marriage Robber

THE ENEMY WITHIN - NEGATIVE THOUGHTS

⁸ And now, dear brothers and sisters, one final thing. Fix your thoughts on what is true, and honourable, and right, and pure, and lovely, and admirable. Think about things that are excellent and worthy of praise

~ Philippians 4:8 (NLT)

I (Kemi) would like to share what God told me a few months ago concerning marriage. There I was, driving into work when I heard a voice whisper to me "Do you know that when you think negatively about your spouse it is a sin?" I thought, "Really? How?" God, in His infinite mercy, began to break it down for me.

Regularly thinking negative thoughts about your spouse increases your dissatisfaction with your spouse and your marriage. There is a scripture that says that the blessing of God makes rich and does not add sorrow. Now when you begin to have regular negative thoughts about your spouse and you entertain them, you are agreeing with the enemy that your marriage is adding sorrow to your life. This will no doubt affect your conduct and how you relate to your spouse.

Every action starts with a thought (e.g., negative thoughts about your spouse) this then leads to a feeling (you become unhappy about your spouse and marriage) which then leads to an action (affects how you relate with your spouse).

You might think it is impossible not to think negative thoughts about your spouse, especially when you are upset with them. I am not suggesting that these thoughts will never come; it is what you do when they do that will determine whether it is a problem or not. The Bible says that out of the abundance of the heart the mouth speaks, if you entertain these thoughts when they come, rather than praying about them or rejecting them, you have made the choice to believe the lies of the devil as opposed to the word of God.

A strong marriage cannot be built by focusing on your spouse's weaknesses; thinking and meditating on them only magnifies them and is not a faith-building exercise.

One of my favourite scriptures is Philippians 4:8. Why would God be so concerned about our thought lives? I think God must know that our thoughts shape our world, even in our marriage. We have to make a daily choice to be thankful by focusing on our spouse's great qualities (strengths). By doing this we are expressing gratitude to God, which in turn affects our attitude towards our spouse. This heart of gratitude and love expressed to God, in turn, flows into our relationship with our spouse.

Heart2Heart
What negative thoughts about your spouse do you need to let go of? Make a list of your spouse's strengths and share it with them. (Discuss)

Prayer
Ask God for forgiveness and thank Him for your spouse and marriage.

The Blame Game

⁵ You hypocrite, first take the plank out of your own eye, and then you will see clearly to remove the speck from your brother's eye

~ Matthew 7:5 (NLT)

It is sometimes easier to focus on blaming our spouses when things are not going the way we thought they should. With every situation, we face we can either choose to react or respond. Reacting is a spontaneous action that has not been thought through. Responding is thinking through your actions to get a result that is to the benefit of your relationship.

A response is when I think of the outcome I want and then act accordingly with restraint rather than when I react without thinking about the outcome. For example, if Kemi speaks to me in a manner I (Bode) consider to be disrespectful, I can choose to respond to her by not reacting in a way that exacerbates the matter but in a way that diffuses the situation and express my hurt rather than lash out in anger.

I (Bode) find that I am much more detailed and painstaking in my approach to things so when we are faced with a situation that throws up the fact that Kemi has not been painstaking, I am more likely to want to blame her rather than seek to resolve the matter. Also, as the saver in our relationship, when it seems that we are running low on funds, I am more likely to take on an approach that Kemi perceives to be questioning and accusatory as I am better at managing the finances in lean times.

Not acting the way I feel requires a lot of self-restraint from me.

Our enemy is the accuser and when we blame our spouse rather than take responsibility for our actions in a situation, we are inadvertently cooperating with the enemy.

Heart2Heart
In what ways do I blame my spouse? (Reflect individually)

Prayer
Ask God to help you remove the log in your eye.

Make Every Day Count

¹⁵ Be very careful, then, how you live — not as unwise but as wise, ¹⁶ making the most of every opportunity, because the days are evil

~ Ephesians 5:15-16 (NIV)

As I (Kemi) think upon this scripture, my mind wanders back to two wedding anniversaries that we lost by not redeeming the time. Yes, we did have an anniversary but the memories are best forgotten, given that we spent them quarrelling with each other. Interestingly, I cannot even remember now what the squabbling was about but I can assure you that it must have been very unimportant. What should have been a wonderful celebration of the gift of love became a painful loss of time that cannot be redeemed.

It is easy to forget that we have an enemy at work, whose mission is to steal, kill and destroy. Sometimes he does it in such subtle ways that we do not realise he has stolen from us, and setting couples against each other is one of his favourite tricks. We can choose to allow him to steal our joy and delight in each other, or we can resist his schemes and "turn the other cheek" rather than choosing to react. Like the scripture says, a gentle answer turns away wrath (Proverbs15:1).

As a result of those lost anniversaries, we agreed that we would work together to eliminate any opportunity the enemy seeks to steal our time and joy from us in our marriage. When we sense mounting tension, sometimes laughing together is a good response to douse the impending inferno. We have not always succeeded, but because of that consciousness, we have had many more wonderful wedding anniversaries and other date nights and celebrations with no incidents.

Heart2Heart

Identify the ways that the enemy is stealing your time with each other as a couple e.g., little things that become a bone of contention (Discuss)

Prayer

Pray for God's protection and for the fruit of the Spirit to be manifest in your marriage.

Investments in Your Marriage

A THREE-FOLD CORD

⁹ Two are better than one because they have a more satisfying return for their labour; ¹⁰ for if either of them falls, the one will lift up his companion. But woe to him who is alone when he falls and does not have another to lift him up. ¹¹ Again, if two lie down together, then they keep warm; but how can one be warm alone? ¹² And though one can overpower him who is alone, two can resist him. A cord of three strands is not quickly broken

~ Ecclesiastes 4:9-12 (NIV)

Whilst dating prior to marriage, attention and excitement seems to be the name of the game, focusing on what we have in common. However once married the reality and the demands of life set in and if we do not pay careful attention to our relationship the novelty wears off. Instead of enjoying the benefits of opposites attracting, the lenses change and the focus shifts to the differences between each other, with each spouse trying to resist and change the other, an exercise that leads to frustration and futility.

In the early days of our marriage whilst trying to make the necessary adjustments that married life brings and getting used to each other, resolving conflicts as a result of the noticeable differences between us posed a real challenge for us. I (Bode) had a phrase which I always relied on to get us focused on the challenge or issue rather than blaming each other, and would often find that I had to repeat it over and over again. The phrase was simply; we are on the same side!

This statement used to irk my wife a lot in those days, looking back now she recognises that the reason it annoyed her was that she felt that agreeing we were on the same side would mean she had failed to prove her point. Being right/victorious was more important to her – as with every human being- than being at peace.

Rather than seeking to win, couples need to seek a win-win situation whenever issues and challenges arise. In a marriage, the goal is never about winning at the expense of our spouse but winning together. It also means no issue is ever really about me but it is always about us. There is nothing more deadly in a marriage than competition. Competition in a marriage simply means that you are competing against yourself. Think about it. When this happens, who wins? At the end of the day, you lose.

Over time, as we both learned how to love each other and work through our differences more constructively, Kemi came to prize our unity over her victory. These days, one of her favourite quips is "winning is overrated and anyway, the price is not worth it for your marriage!"

Victory in marriage is being there for each other and covering each other's nakedness so that together we are stronger. One thing that is needed more than ever in marriage is camaraderie. The natural human instinct is to go after our own desires and wants but God is always looking for a heart that seeks to do right by Him, having God at the heart of our relationship gives us the right perspective, and helps us keep the equilibrium and balance right. As we look to Him and draw from His strength, we can lay down our desires and take on his selfless and loving nature; a love that seeks to give. Having done this, we are able to love our spouses in return, but without this, we cannot walk together in agreement.

Heart2Heart
In what ways can you better support each other? Can you come up with a phrase like ours that can help you to regain perspective

when you're in an argument? (Discuss)

Prayer
Pray that God will be at the centre of your relationship.

WEEK 32

Investments in Your Marriage
PRAYER: THE BEST GIFT YOU CAN GIVE

⁹ Two are better than one because they have a more satisfying return for their labour; ¹⁰ for if either of them falls, the one will lift up his companion. But woe to him who is alone when he falls and does not have another to lift him up. ¹¹ Again, if two lie down together, then they keep warm; but how can one be warm alone? ¹² And though one can overpower him who is alone, two can resist him. A cord of three strands is not quickly broken

~ Ecclesiastes 4:9-12 (NIV)

The best gift that we can give our spouse is our prayers. God has a purpose for all of His creation and prayer is the key to unlocking God's purpose for our lives. Prayer is the way through which our spirit connects with God's spirit, and allows Him to fill our hearts with His plans and purposes and equip us with the strength to do His will.

Praying for your spouse helps to align their will to God's, scheduling their seasons to fit into the appointed time of God's will. This alignment allows God's favour, protection, mercy, grace, forgiveness and all of His promises to become a reality in your spouse's life.

By committing your spouse into God's hands, you ensure that they are secure in His care and show your dependence on Him. He is able to strengthen your spouse so that they can be obedient to His will in their conduct, choices and decisions as they continue on life's journey. Praying for your spouse and relationship allows you to invite God into your marriage and is the key to a successful marriage. We are all imperfect and marriage is a very spiritual journey. God uses our experiences to grow and mature us into becoming more like Him if we allow Him. By increasing the spiritual atmosphere in our homes through prayer we enhance our ability to function the way God intended in our daily relationship with our spouse. Throughout our life's journey, we have been and continue to be encouraged and strengthened by praying for each other; covering each other's "nakedness" spiritually.

In April 2005, I (Kemi) was involved in a major car accident on my way to a hospital appointment during my pregnancy. Prior to leaving the house in the morning, Bode had prayed for me and with me as was his usual custom. I am certain that the timely prayer averted the enemy's plans because, despite the severity of the accident, both I and the baby were completely unharmed.

Praying for your spouse is a necessity.

Heart2Heart
Share your prayer needs with your spouse, both the big things and the small ones. (Discuss)

Prayer
Pray for your spouse and ask God to make you an intercessor for your spouse.

Investments in Your Marriage

PRAYING TOGETHER

⁹ Two are better than one because they have a more satisfying return for their labour; ¹⁰ for if either of them falls, the one will lift up his companion. But woe to him who is alone when he falls and does not have another to lift him up. ¹¹ Again, if two lie down together, then they keep warm; but how can one be warm alone? ¹² And though one can overpower him who is alone, two can resist him. A cord of three strands is not quickly broken

~ Ecclesiastes 4:9-12 (NIV)

We are all imperfect and marriage is a spiritual journey. God uses our experiences to grow and mature us into becoming more like Him if we allow Him. By increasing the spiritual atmosphere in our homes through prayer we enhance our ability to function the way God intended in our daily relationship with our spouse.

In the context of marriage, prayer is very important. Prayer brings clarity and allows the Holy Spirit to be the pilot of the relationship. It strengthens the marriage and provides a proper foundation on which to build. Studies have shown that less than 8% of Christian couples actually engage in prayer together, which could be the reason why many marriages are unable to weather the challenges they encounter.

God is the creator of marriage and each individual. He under-stands each individual's behaviour, personality and feelings. When we are mutually submitted to Him, we have access to the deeper and "unsearchable" wisdom about each other and our experiences which His Spirit provides (Jeremiah 33:3 "Call to me and I will answer you and tell you great and unsearchable things you do not know"). We have the assurance that once we have God on our side we are better equipped with the necessary skills and traits to address our relational, emotional and behavioural issues with Godly balance.

God gave your spouse to you and vice versa. He already knows all the issues that may arise during the marriage. (He knows the end from the beginning) it is therefore very wise to commit every aspect of your marriage to Him and to be mutually submitted to Him. When a couple engages in an active and healthy prayer life together, their marriage encounters a number of benefits.

Heartfelt prayer brings us into God's presence and opens our spiritual eyes, enabling us to see ourselves as we really are. Our imperfections become obvious to us and our motives are laid bare before us. This shifts our individual focus to God and away from each other's frailties leading to personal change, greater patience, deeper compassion, better understanding and unconditional love for the other which serves to benefit the marriage relationship.

Benefits of Praying Together
- Gives you access to the power of agreement (Matthew 18:19).
- Fosters unity in your relationship as you learn to be vulnerable with each other before God (Psalms 133).
- Promotes accountability and intimacy as you both learn to bring your deepest thoughts and desires before God.
- Has a positive influence on your children as they are exposed to the reality of a loving, faithful and dependable God and helps to sow the seeds of a rich relationship with Him as they grow up into adults.

Heart2Heart
Identify ways you can improve your prayer times together. (Discuss)

Prayer
Ask God to pour out His spirit of grace and intercession upon you as a couple.

Keeping The Flames of Love Alive

⁶ Place me like a seal over your heart, like a seal on your arm; for love is as strong as death, its jealousy unyielding as the grave. It burns like blazing fire, like a mighty flame. ⁷ Many waters cannot quench love; rivers cannot sweep it away. If one were to give all the wealth of one's house for love, it would be utterly scorned

~ Song of Solomon 8:6-7 (NIV)

What is it with our generation that we seem to have lost the joy of savouring moments and building beautiful memories? Today's microwave mentality seems to incline everyone to live life in such a hurry, with all manner of drive-throughs and quick-fix solutions provided to pander to our ever-shortening capacity for patience.

As I (Bode) reflect on today's frenetic pace of life, I think about how easy it is to get so caught up in the demands of life that we fail to continually invest in our love for each other, where and when it matters the most. There are different seasons in marriage: in some, we will experience fewer romantic feelings; in others, we may have less opportunity to do or say things that leave a positive deposit of love and affection for each other.

Three Greek words convey the dimensions of love that need to exist in a marriage if it is to remain healthy and wholesome. They are; agape, phileo and eros. Agape is God's unconditional love, phileo is a love born out of deep friendship, and eros is a love characterised by a deep passion for each other. Now, there may be seasons in a marriage where one dimension of love is more prevalent than the others, but all three need to exist in a marriage for a fulfilling marriage experience.

Consider for a moment what a marriage without eros i.e., without passion and romance, would feel and look like? Clearly, it will soon succumb to a boring, frustrating existence. God has created us all with a desire to be intimate and romance has a way of making what could have been a humdrum existence very exciting. When I (Bode) reflect back on our marriage, the times that we have set apart to do romantic things have gone a long way in helping us build intimacy in our marriage especially as work demands mean that I am sometimes working away from home for extended periods of time.

Regardless of the actual time spent in each other's presence, what helps to nurture our relationship, are the times that we have set apart to do romantic things. These times have gone a long way in helping us build intimacy in our marriage. During the times that we have inadvertently failed to carve out exclusive time to fan the flames of our romance, we have found ourselves feeling remote and distant from each other despite being together twenty-four seven. Investing time in romantic experiences make the times that we are together now even more special and planning these romantic experiences gives us something to look forward to.

Your marriage is in need of romance so give it your time. You will find it's one of the best decisions you will ever make.

Heart2Heart
Identify ways you can improve your prayer times together. (Discuss)

Prayer
Ask God to pour out His spirit of grace and intercession upon you as a couple.

Deposits in Your Love Bank

PART 1

⁹ Let us not become weary in doing good, for at the proper time we will reap a harvest if we do not give up

~ Galatians 6:9 (NIV)

Marriage is like a plant; in order to keep it growing and healthy, it needs to be looked after. Often times in our marriage, it is the little daily acts of love that make a huge difference. As we go through the humdrum of everyday life it is easy to neglect our marriage relationship, forgetting to plant the "seeds of love", being affectionate towards each other outside of the bedroom, being kind towards each other, saying hello, thank you and please.

It is easy to assume that your spouse knows you love them, so you do not need to tell them, but remember that your affection cannot be left to speculation. Telling your spouse how you feel about them reassures them. The world beyond the walls of your home can be a less than loving place and your words go a long way in acting as a gentle reminder, keeping the scent of your love ever fresh. In order to build a lifelong marriage, we need to find out what matters to our spouses and once we know it; act upon what we know. I (Kemi) know that the words that I speak to Bode mean a lot to him, I am constantly looking for opportunities to affirm him and tell him just how much I appreciate his kind-hearted and selfless nature.

I (Bode) make time to listen to Kemi as she pours out her heart to me and shares her many ideas of changing the world. Use your words and actions to build your marriage.

Heart2Heart
In what ways can you put love deposits into your marriage? Do something this week for your spouse that will count as a deposit. (Discuss)

Prayer
Ask God to show you how you can care and love your spouse more.

Deposits in Your Love Bank

PART 2

[11] A man's wisdom gives him patience; it is to his glory to overlook an offense

~ Proverbs 19:11 (NIV)

As a couple living and interacting with each other on a daily basis, we will often hurt our dearest and best unintentionally. It is easy to allow a standoff where each person is waiting for the other to apologise, resulting in a loss of precious time. When we do not make up quickly, we miss out on enjoying each other's company.

Marriage is a gift from God and it is important that we do not allow the enemy to steal from us. Learning to say sorry often and quickly goes a long way in ensuring we live in harmony. It is wise and humble to forgo an offence for the sake of your marriage. Make a choice to walk away from strife. In marriage opportunities for conflict arise constantly, what makes the difference is our choice to either overlook them or resolve them in an appropriate, Christ-like manner, rather than making it a battle of wills.

It is important that we make a choice to respond and not react, not allowing our emotions to take over but allowing the Holy Spirit to flow through us. Being right is overrated and having a harmonious, strife free home is far more important.

By making a decision to overlook an offence by your spouse, you are making a deposit into your love bank. Choose life.

Heart2Heart

Are you holding any hurt against your spouse? Is there anything you need to share with each other? An offence that needs to be overlooked? A sensitive issue that needs to be discussed? (Discuss)

Prayer

Ask God for His help to let go of any hurt you might have against your spouse.

Deposits in Your Love Bank

PART 3

> [9] *Whoever would foster love covers over an offense, but whoever repeats the matter separates close friends*
>
> ~ Proverbs 17:9 (NIV)

In our interactions with each other, we will hurt and be hurt by each other as we are human and our expectations may not be met at times, resulting in us getting upset. It helps to remember that forgiveness is an important component of a healthy marriage as there will be times when we might need to be forgiven or offer forgiveness.

We know from scriptures that to maintain our own spiritual health, it is crucial that we understand and embrace the power of forgiveness. The seventy times seven principle was not a burden placed on us by God, it is actually a gift from Him that we give to ourselves when we obey the command to forgive.

Forgiveness ensures that the drains of everyday interaction remain clear and unblocked so the pipes continue to give passage to a smooth flow between us as husband and wife. Intimacy happens where there is trust, honesty and openness, unresolved hurt eats away at the foundation of intimacy.

True forgiveness is not pretending that something did not happen but it is a choice to set your spouse free from their debt (hurt caused to you), letting go of resentment and vengeance.

Forgiveness is God's command and it is an act that requires us to give up the right to punish. A successful marriage is a "Union of forgivers".

Heart2Heart
Identify any issue that you may need to ask or give forgiveness for. (Discuss)

Prayer
Pray that you will always have a forgiving spirit towards each other.

Deposits in Your Love Bank

PART 4

⁴ Love is patient, love is kind. It does not envy, it does not boast, it is not proud

~ 1 Corinthians 13:4 (NIV)

²² But the fruit of the Spirit is love, joy, peace, longsuffering, kindness, goodness, faithfulness

~ Galatians 5:22 (NIV)

Marriage presents an opportunity for us to become more Christ-like. My (Kemi's) patience has been and continues to be tested as part of my daily walk with the Lord. I am not the most patient person, I will admit, I seem to live life in the fast lane whilst Bode is patient and enjoys savouring the moments. I hate being late, as I consider it to be disrespectful and a negative character trait. Bode on the other hand likes to take his time (better late than never).

At the start of our marriage, I used to get so worked up in the mornings if we were running late. Prior to getting married, I could count the number of times I was late for anything in my life, getting married changed all that. Sunday mornings came with a slight irritation as I would sometimes get to church late and would need a few minutes to compose myself due to my conduct on the way. When I reflect back now, it seems so ironic that in my mind the pursuit of God by arriving at church early was more important than living out my Christian faith in my dealings with Bode. My impatience, irritation and anger when we were running late certainly cancelled my moral stance and my timekeeping strength as it was at the expense of our relationship. Instead of feeling anger at how I would be perceived by others for getting to church late, I should have been thinking of how I could lovingly help Bode with his timekeeping, and continue to show respect to him regardless. My need for punctuality must never be at the expense of loving my husband. Yes, we are called to help harness our strengths and minimise our weaknesses but we are required to do so in a loving and God-honouring way.

My deposits in our love bank have involved seeking to understand my husband by being more patient and supporting him in his area of weakness, choosing to act in love especially when his area of weakness is an area of strength for me.

Whilst I (Kemi) am not excusing his lateness, helping him by giving him a little nudge the night before, and timely reminders of when we need to leave the house and arrive at our outing have made a huge difference in living in peace and harmony. Bode on the other hand continues to put deposits in our love bank by being gentle, reassuring and patient with me when I am in a hurry, anxious and impatient.

After all, the fruit of the Spirit is patience, not timeliness – I have recognised that I need to value what God values and do what His Spirit empowers me to do, not strive to conform Bode to what I think is right.

Heart2Heart
In what ways do you need to show patience to your spouse? (Discuss)

Prayer
Ask God for the fruit of the Spirit to be evident in your relationship with each other. Ask His Holy Spirit to empower you to be patient.

Enjoying Your Wife

¹⁸ May your fountain be blessed, and may you rejoice in the wife of your youth.

~ Proverbs 5:18 (NLT)

We spend our courtship days seeking what will make each other happy, discovering the joy of new experiences together while finding out what makes each other tick. We spend our time doing what the other will appreciate as we seek to make deposits into our "love bank".

When we get married, if we are not intentional about our relationship, the routines and familiarity of daily life take over and we resign ourselves to seeking other pleasures.

There is no pleasure quite as enjoyable as doing things together as a couple. Planning and making this happen can be challenging initially but our determination and commitment will go a long way to ensuring it happens and the rewards will be worth the effort.

Casting our minds back to our courtship days when we enjoyed doing things together, helps us realise that now our mental attitudes have changed; we want to have our own way, do our own things, isn't that interesting? Knowing that God desires us to love sacrificially rather than conditionally can be of much help at these times!

The phrase rejoicing in the wife of your youth depicts intentionality about appreciating and celebrating our love for each other, for wine connoisseurs tell us that wine gets better with age. That is exactly how the celebration of our love for each other should get with age.

Your marriage is strengthened when you spend time with your spouse, listening to each other and enjoying each other's company reminiscing about your shared experiences and life together

Heart2Heart
In what ways can you celebrate your love? When was the last time you went on a date and reminisced about your days of courtship? Why not arrange a date with your spouse? (Discuss)

Prayer
Thank God for the gift of your marriage and ask Him to help you not take each other for granted.

Speaking The Truth in Love

15 Instead, speaking the truth in love, we will in all things grow up into him who is the Head, that is Christ.

~ Ephesians 4:15 (BSB)

18 Do not let any unwholesome talk come out of your mouths, but only what is helpful for building others up according to their needs, that it may benefit those who listen.

~ Ephesians 4:29 (NIV)

We are reminded to speak the truth in love; this requires tact and wisdom. Sometimes I (Kemi) find that what I meant to say is not what I said, or the way I said it was not how I meant it, leading to needless hurt and pain.

We are encouraged in the scripture above to think about the words that we speak so that it is coming from a place of love, saying what we mean and meaning what we say. Being truthful requires us to be sensitive and kind to our spouse, especially when it involves dealing with a difficult situation such as giving negative feedback on their behaviour.

It is always helpful to check our motives prior to having a discussion to ensure that it is coming from a place of love rather than a place of anger, a place of reconciliation rather than a place of retaliation. It is important that you communicate the good things you love about your spouse often so that when you need to speak about the more challenging areas of their behaviour they are assured of your love and acceptance.

I (Kemi) recall a difficult conversation recently that I needed to have with Bode about an area that needed work on, whilst it was not an easy conversation when I (Bode) reflected on it, I had a good laugh as I realised that if this conversation had happened in the early days of our marriage, it would have been a different outcome. I (Kemi) am learning to use the sandwich approach, starting with a positive comment, then negative feedback and ending with a positive comment.

I also think carefully about my choice of words and the outcome that I would like at the end of the conversation more than I would in the early years of marriage when I would dive in and just say what I thought without any care or concern about Bode's feelings. I remember a particular conflict where Bode said to me; "What makes you think everyone wants a piece of your mind? If you keep giving a piece of your mind, there will be nothing left at this rate."

Heart2Heart
In what ways do you need to change your communication style to reflect truth and grace? What truth do you need to speak to each other? (Discuss)

Prayer
Ask God and your spouse for forgiveness for the times that you have not spoken the truth in love.

Responding to Change

PART 1

¹ There is a time for everything, and a season for every activity under the heavens: ² a time to be born and a time to die, a time to plant and a time to uproot, ³ a time to kill and a time to heal, a time to tear down and a time to build, ⁴ a time to weep and a time to laugh, a time to mourn and a time to dance, ⁵ a time to scatter stones and a time to gather them, a time to embrace and a time to refrain from embracing, ⁶ a time to search and a time to give up, a time to keep and a time to throw away, ⁷ a time to tear and a time to mend, a time to be silent and a time to speak, ⁸ a time to love and a time to hate, a time for war and a time for peace

~ Ecclesiastes 3:1-8 (NIV)

It is interesting to note that wherever we turn in the world today, the only constant is change. As I (Kemi) peer out of the windows at home, I see that change is happening all around me.

Apart from ushering in cold and windy weather, the autumn season is gradually displacing the glorious sunshine which I have enjoyed and become accustomed to. The warmth and brightness of summer has been the dominant theme of my daily experience over the past few months; light clothing... numerous colours, blossoming flowers...you get the picture.

As I ponder on this, I am made aware of the fact that it will only get colder and gradually less of the sun will be seen as the months go by.

It then dawned on me that what I see is the first stirrings of a new season; a new beginning. It is exciting to see change happen right before my eyes, but I know that if I had been given a choice, I wouldn't have chosen to leave the warm and sunny climate I had been experiencing over the past few months.

Like the challenges that the changes in weather bring everyone's way, we all have to expect new challenges as new seasons or new beginnings and circumstances beyond our control, are ushered into our lives by God. There is no place where this is more apparent than the marriage relationship. In essence; what you experience from the moment you say "I do", will be determined in many ways by how you respond to the changes that come your way.

Heart2Heart
How are you responding to changes in your marriage journey? What changes do you need to accept in each other? (Discuss)

Prayer
Ask God to help you remain faithful to your spouse through the changing scenes of life and circumstances.

Responding to Change

PART 2

¹ Therefore, I urge you, brothers and sisters, in view of God's mercy, to offer your bodies as a living sacrifice, holy and pleasing to God – this is your true and proper worship. ² Do not conform to the pattern of this world, but be transformed by the renewing of your mind. Then you will be able to test and approve what God's will is – his good, pleasing and perfect will

~ Romans 12:1-2 (NIV)

Let us take a look at the impact which changes around us can have on our marriage experience. Can we determine the outcome of these changes in our relationship? Do we have a personal role to play in ensuring that our marriage grows stronger through these changing circumstances? Are we at the mercy of these circumstances? We have heard it said many times from the pulpit that the spiritual realm governs the events we experience in the physical realm, so in this instance, can we in any way influence the spiritual realm to affect the physical experiences we have in our marriage?

For many of us who have been through various challenging experiences since the day we said "I do", the questions above are certainly not easy to answer. Marriage in itself is a relational experience involving two individuals who have previously had a variety of different experiences. These experiences have resulted in a complex web of outcomes influencing everything from our personalities to the way we think, act, speak, see things and interpret what we go through every day. The result of all this is that the probability that both of us will respond the same way to any given experience is very remote. Basically, the inner working of our emotional interaction with the environment around us, though manageable, is quite a complex one.

We also realise that much as we would love that it wasn't so, we live in an imperfect world. A world that influences our daily experiences in all areas of life including our marriage and throws situations that constantly challenge our feelings, values, faith and conduct as we wake up to each new day.

When we consider the complex influences on marriages today, it is clear that we cannot address the questions above by drawing purely on the way we see our daily experiences. For one, we would all see it differently as everyone seems to be coming from a different place, a different background, a different societal class, a different culture, a different gender makeup, different level and type of education and different experiences in life. The list goes on.

God has provided direction for us through His Word, a timeless manual for all the changing scenes of life. Our attitude to change depends on our thinking patterns... our thinking patterns about life, about the nature of the environment we live in, about the word of the Lord's prophets, about the psychology of relationships and everyday life, about the nature of the world we live in and the numerous opportunities for differing opinion and about our belief in the timeless nature (or otherwise) of God's word in the context of all the above.

Could it be that God is asking each of us to stop looking at the circumstances that are the evidence of changes taking place around us and to focus rather on how our minds process these events? The Bible gives us a clear picture to illustrate this in the book of Proverbs when it says, "as a man thinketh, so is he" (KJV).

Arguably more than what we profess with our mouths, what we believe in our hearts and think every day will shape the experiences we have in life (and in our marriages) to a very significant degree.

Heart2Heart
What mindset do you have about your marriage that needs to change? (Discuss)

Prayer
Ask God to help you have the right kingdom mindset for your marriage.

WEEK 43

Blended Gifts

² He created them male and female and blessed them. And he named them 'Mankind' when they were created

~ Genesis 5:2 (NIV)

Differences are part of God's purpose for our marriage; evident in the way He created Adam and Eve in the beginning. His intention is that our differences help us complement each other. I (Kemi) cannot believe just how different Bode and I are; he is a good saver and I am a great spender, he takes his time to do things and is detail-oriented and I am ready to get on with it; he adheres to speed limits as they are there for our benefit (better late than never) and I am always in a hurry wanting to get to where I am going early even when there is no urgency; he loves to go to art galleries, taking in the beauty, and I love to go to the theatre and play my music loudly.

Needless to say that when we got married, a lot of adjustments needed to be made! Some days into our marriage during our honeymoon I was shocked to discover that Bode was happy staying in the hotel lounging rather than being out there exploring the beautiful sights of our honeymoon destination. The man of my dreams was not really as I thought. There were many more shocking revelations as our differences became more obvious.

He liked to get up early to pray; I liked to take my time getting up and praying. I liked to process things in my mind before discussing them; he liked to get things out in the open and deal with them immediately.

Most marriages are made up of opposites, as opposites attract. Blended gifts is about embracing the gift of our spouse, celebrating and appreciating our differences and enjoying the diversity and the richness it brings into our world. As couples, we cannot effectively deal with the issues of life without embracing and celebrating our differences. When we approach issues with an open perspective, considering our spouse's opinions, thoughts and ideas we are likely to get a better result.

Our differences are not mistakes but a divine opportunity to expose us to situations that enhance us by showing us another way of being; leading to personal growth.

Heart2Heart
List five differences between you and your spouse. How can these differences make your marriage more balanced and complete? (Discuss)

Prayer
Ask God to open your eyes to the benefits that your differences bring to your marriage.

Money Talks

28 Suppose one of you wants to build a tower. Won't you first sit down and estimate the cost to see if you have enough money to complete it? 29 For if you lay the foundation and are not able to finish it, everyone who sees it will ridicule you

~ Luke 14:28-29 (NIV)

Shared financial building and planning can be a key element to bonding within your marriage. Every couple needs a plan for their finances. Without a plan, we are likely to fail to realise, accomplish or bring to fruition our financial dreams, ambitions, wishes and aspirations.

Without a realistic perspective on money, financial issues can cause more problems for couples than almost any other thing within a marriage. The problem usually is not the actual finances but is related to the underlying value system each person has.

Your ability to manage and steward your finances will be determined by your attitude towards money which is informed by your value system, previous experiences, culture, knowledge, upbringing and understanding.

We all have differing opinions and attitudes about money and this can have a devastating effect on the marriage relationship if assumptions are made and your differences are not talked through, understood and blended together well. Our differences should bring balance and not chaos.

Remember that money is not the first or even the second priority in happy people's lives – the Bible teaches us that the love of money is the root of all kinds of evil. (1 Timothy 6:10)

Your health, relationships with family and friends, career satisfaction and fulfilling interests are more important, so put money in the right place in your relationship.

Heart2Heart
How are you building financial intimacy in your marriage? (Discuss your attitude towards money)

Prayer
Ask for God's help in managing the differences in your approach to your finances and for you to be good stewards.

Knowing You, Knowing Me

12 Therefore, as God's chosen people, holy and dearly loved, clothe yourselves with compassion, kindness, humility, gentleness and patience

~ Colossians 3:12 (NIV)

During our second year of marriage, we went on the Marriage Course at Holy Trinity Church, Brompton (HTB). Kemi had suggested that we should attend and I (Bode), who was very passionate about relationships and an advocate for marriage, thought that attending the course would be another step towards building on our already good marriage.

The course ran for eight weeks with talks interspersed with exercises that you completed with your spouse and discussed as a couple. On the first day of the course, I (Bode) was very much "humbled" when we got to our first exercise, called "Knowing you, knowing me". We each had to choose three out of a list of sixteen areas that mattered to us most. Having completed that, we were then required to choose three out of the same list that we thought mattered most to our spouse. At the end of the exercise, we had a discussion to ascertain just how well we understood each other.

When it was time to discuss our answers, I (Bode) was certain that I had got Kemi's top three priorities right, but in fact, I had only got one out of the three! I (Kemi) got two out of Bode's three top priorities right. This was an eye-opener as we both realised that we did not know each other as much as we thought we did.

That experience taught us that it is important not to assume we know what our spouse needs, but rather we need to listen and take in the things our spouse tells us (in words and in deeds).

Dissatisfaction in marriage sometimes arises as a result of one person feeling that their needs are not being met, while their spouse thinks they are doing their best to meet their spouse's needs.

Heart2Heart
Ask your spouse what they need from you at this time. Discuss. (Suggestions on areas to consider include Acceptance, Sexual Intimacy, Affirmation, Security, Romance etc)

Prayer
Ask God to help you meet your spouse's needs.

Expressions of Love

PART 1

⁷ Many waters cannot quench love; rivers cannot sweep it away. If one were to give all the wealth of one's house for love, it would be utterly scorned

~ Song of Solomon 8:7 (NIV)

I am certain that you will agree with me that the word, "love" is one of the most used yet most misunderstood words in the world. We start our marriage with the promise to love one another, however as the years go by we find that loving our spouse against all odds becomes a big challenge as our ability to stay in love is constantly tested.

1 Corinthians 13:1-8 is always a good starting point for us when we encounter challenges in loving our spouses. Love in a marriage is being committed irrevocably to give all that we have to meeting the needs of our partner, unconditionally. This is a love that is marked by giving, not seeking to get. In order to love this way, we need the help of the Holy Spirit as we cannot do it in our own strength. The kind of love that God is calling us to in our marriages is one that is more than emotions, feelings, attraction, and chemistry; it requires a conscious decision to keep the vows that were made to each other in the presence of God on the wedding day.

Unconditional love is important in a marriage relationship. This is the love that God wants us to have for our spouses, it is God's love for us and acceptance of us that makes us love him more and seek to please Him in all our ways.

This is the way that God expects us to love our spouses, if we withhold our affection because of our spouse's weaknesses, then our love is selfish, motivated only by our satisfaction, and will not work.

Heart2Heart
How can you show commitment to your spouse? (Discuss)

Prayer
Ask God to help you love your spouse the way he loves you.

Expressions of Love

PART 2

⁷ Many waters cannot quench love; rivers cannot sweep it away. If one were to give all the wealth of one's house for love, it would be utterly scorned

~ Song of Solomon 8:7 (NIV)

It is important that our love for our spouse is communicated not only by our words but also with consistent, appropriate and convincing actions. 1 John 3:18 states "Dear children, let's not merely say that we love each other; let us show the truth by our actions." As a spouse, finding out your spouse's 'love language' will help you love them in a manner that will communicate to them through your actions that you love them.

Gary Chapman identified five ways of receiving and expressing love. Each of us uses all of them at different times, but we usually have one or two that communicate love more strongly to us than the others. The five love languages are:

- **Words of Affirmation:** This is when you say how nice your spouse looks, or how great the dinner tasted. These words will also build your mate's self-image and confidence.

- **Quality Time:** Some feel most loved when you simply spend time with them, being together, doing things together, and focusing on one another. If this is your partner's love language, turn off the TV, and give them some undivided attention.

- **Gifts:** Gifts don't have to be expensive to send a powerful message of love, just thoughtful. Spouses who forget a birthday or anniversary or who never give gifts to someone whose primary way of expressing and receiving love is gift-giving will find themselves with a spouse who feels neglected and unloved.

- **Acts of Service:** Discovering how you can best do something for your spouse will require time and creativity. These acts of service like vacuuming, hanging a bird feeder, planting a garden, etc., need to be done with joy in order to be perceived as a gift of love.

- **Physical Touch:** Sometimes just stroking your spouse's back, holding hands, or a peck on the cheek will fulfil this need.

Expressing love to your spouse in a way that they can best receive it is important. Love your spouse the way he or she best feels loved, not the way you want to be loved.

Heart2Heart
Discuss your love language with each other. How can you go about making your spouse feel deeply loved this week?

Prayer
Ask God to help you love your spouse the way they want to be loved and for you to be able to meet their needs.

WEEK 48

A Godly Heritage

26 Those who fear the Lord are secure; he will be a refuge for their children

~ Proverbs 14:26 (NLT)

Children learn about God from their parents. I (Kemi) remember when our son turned two. It was a challenging time for me as he constantly threw tantrums and tried to assert himself. If you are a mum or dad reading this piece, you have probably heard about the "terrible two" phase. After a particularly difficult week with him, I suddenly realised I had become more like a child in my approach to him and this only added to my frustration.

The Holy Spirit reminded me that my actions towards my son would be a major influence on his salvation, even at his tender age, and that I needed to change my approach to relating with him and begin to see him more through the eyes of God. He was after all a gift and responsibility handed to me by God as my stewardship to Him. Even though I had heard this before, because God said it directly to me at a difficult period, it sank deep into my consciousness, changed my life, and has continued to inform my relationship with my son to this day.

As I began to realise that more than my words, my conduct spoke volumes to my son, our relationship was gradually improved. Since then, I have marvelled at how God has changed our relationship and how He is working in me to build a more fruitful relationship with this little individual (now in his teenage years) who is so precious in His eyes.

My son's questions to me about why things are the way they are have also reinforced my belief that my interactions with him will strongly influence his view of God and the need for salvation as he learns what God is like from me. If I am patient and kind and slow to anger, he will be more inclined to find out more about a God like that than he would if he sees me as an impatient mum or one who is constantly angry or snapping at him.

When he was younger, I recall a conversation with him on our way to his school. He had asked me why we pray every time to a Jesus who is not physically present (His words were "Why do we pray to Jesus who is not here?") I took a deep breath, asked God for help, and said to him, "Yes, he is in your heart".

Not satisfied with my response, He said; "But I cannot see him." I then said, "Remember how every morning on the way to school you ask me, "Mum please can I get some fresh air?" and I say yes? Do you ever see the fresh air come into the car as the windows come down?" "No mummy," he said. "But how then do you know it has come into the car?" I asked. He said, "I just know it." Then I said to him, "It is exactly the same, Jesus is with us even though we do not see Him."

These little seeds sown, I pray will germinate and result in him being a soul winner someday.

Heart2Heart
How can you help your children build their relationship with God? (Discuss)

Prayer
Ask God for wisdom to recognise opportunities that He offers you to help your child/children grow in their faith in God.

WEEK 49

Your Legacy

⁴ Fathers, do not exasperate your children; instead, bring them up in the training and instruction of the Lord

~ Ephesians 6:4 (NIV)

Our children are watching us and observing our conduct towards each other. Our actions speak much louder than our words, and their marriages will be shaped by our marriages. In this day where there is so much negative news and views about marriage and the world's values are seeping into the Church, it is important that we show by example that God designed marriage and marriage is a good thing.

Children need to see mums and dads who love each other and are committed to each other.

Some years ago, we were surprised when our six-year-old son asked us about his marriage; when he can get married, and to whom? We had a good laugh but realised that because he is surrounded by so many couples with good marriages in church, his mind is being shaped towards wanting and expecting a strong marriage. The choices you make today have great ramifications for the destinies of your children. There are so many stories in the Bible that shed some light on the importance of our legacy. A study of Timothy and his faith and David and his family in the Bible highlights the importance of this even more.

Choices that you make and actions that you take now with regards to how you treat each other will determine how your children treat their spouses.

Heart2Heart

How would you want your children to describe your marriage? What can you do to make it happen? (Discuss)

Prayer

Pray that your marriage will stand the test of time and be a legacy for your children. Pray that their marriages will be strong too.

.

Praying For Your Child

16b The prayer of a righteous person is powerful and effective

~ James 5:16b (NIV)

As the scripture above illustrates, there is power in godly couples praying and prayer is the greatest gift that we can give to our children. Our children are gifts from God and we act as stewards over their lives. I (Kemi) have found parenting to be very humbling and challenging as I have had to pray and depend on God for wisdom and self-control.

Prayer offers us an opportunity to be co-labourers with God in shaping and laying tracks for our children's destiny and future. Whilst we do not have control over our children's choices and each will have to make the choice to accept the free gift of salvation when they get to the age of volition, we do have the power to cry out to God on their behalf.

Praying for our children and with our children is important as it gives us a window into their world and concerns and also offers the opportunity to model a life of prayer to them, showing that God is very real in our lives.

Praying for their destinies, character, different phases, and stages of life before they happen is important as it can avert the enemy's traps and protect our children. It is important we pray as couples over and about our children.

Heart2Heart
How can you pray for and with your child/children? What concerns do you have about your child/children? (Discuss)

Prayer
Ask God to help you pray for your child/children and bring those concerns before God..

.

WEEK 51

Lean on Me

20 He who walks with wise men will be wise, But the companion of fools will be destroyed

~ Proverbs 13:20 (NKJV)

During our premarital classes whilst preparing for our upcoming wedding and subsequent marriage, we were encouraged to watch the company we keep and to look for couples who had good marriages and were committed to strengthening their marriages. At the time I (Kemi) wondered why this was so important and strongly emphasised. As the years have gone by, I now fully realise just how valuable this advice was.

On our marriage journey, we have been blessed with friendships with couples who are committed to having strong marriages, some are in our peer groups, some are older couples with many years of marriage behind them and when we hang out with them we glean from the wisdom they share and their actions.

Spending time with couples who share our values has strengthened our marriage, reinforcing our positive view of marriage, and has ensured that our worldview of marriage remains positive and godly. It has also strengthened our resolve to continue to build our marriage and remain committed to each other.

We are fortunate to be part of a loving community in our local church and encourage every couple to look for couples within their church family who are committed to helping them build a strong marriage and when necessary to lean on their pastoral team. Sometimes a couple might go through an issue that requires some external support and godly biblical counselling.

If and when you need this, it is not something to be ashamed of. The earlier you get the counselling, the better.

Struggles do not mean you have failed or are failing, they simply mean you need a helping hand along the way.

Heart2Heart
How can you strengthen your marriage? Who are the couples that help strengthen your marriage? (Discuss)

Prayer
Ask God to bring godly marriage relationships your way.

WEEK 52

Treasures in Heavenly Places

19 Do not store up for yourselves treasures on earth, where moths and vermin destroy, and where thieves break in and steal. 20 But store up for yourselves treasures in heaven, where moths and vermin do not destroy, and where thieves do not break in ands teal. 21For where your treasure is, there your heart will be also

~ Matthew 6:19-21 (NIV)

God has a plan for every marriage He brings together and His desire is that in bringing us together our marriages are building and adding to His kingdom. God brings us together in partnership with Him and each other to fulfil His plans here on earth. Our actions here on earth have a significant impact on our eternal destiny.

Using our time, talent, and treasure as a couple for God, helps us make a difference in the lives of those around us, whether at work, in our neighbourhood, church, or in the life of anyone who has an interaction with us.

Here are some ways to store up treasures in heaven:

- **Make time**
It is important to create time for others and invest in the lives of those around you. Make your home a welcoming place for others and make time to be available for others. An inwardly focused marriage will not be a blessing to others.

- **Be generous**
God blesses us and our marriages and calls us to be generous with

every resource that He sends us. We should not make the mistake of thinking we own or deserve any of the good things we have: God owns them all and gives them to us to steward wisely. Seize every opportunity you get to be generous to others and to share with them.

- **Pray for others**

Praying for others is a great opportunity to be a blessing and to store up treasures in heavenly places.

Heart2Heart

How can your marriage be a godly influence to those around you? How can you use the resources that God has given you to lay up treasures in eternity? (Discuss)

Prayer

Ask God to help you identify opportunities around you to use your marriage to store up treasures in heaven, not just to accumulate treasures on earth.

Closing Thoughts

We trust that the times that you have set apart to seek God in using this devotional together have been fruitful and a great investment in your marriage. Seeking God together will also have helped you grow closer together spiritually and to experience a new dimension of oneness and intimacy.

As you continue on your marriage journey, there are four things we want to encourage you to do, to invest in your marriage: Do fun things together e.g., date nights, walking together, sports together; Continue in prayer together e.g. daily or weekly prayer times together; Laugh together; Book time away with each other;

Marriage is a journey and not a destination. Our prayer for you is that you will experience God's grace throughout the seasons of your marriage journey, be it autumn, spring, summer or winter.

Enjoy and celebrate your love.

In his love and ours,
~ Kemi and Bode Olutunbi ~

CONNECT

WITH US

AT

www.lovetalks.tv

@LOVETALKSTV

Kemi and Bode are a husband and wife team who do life together at home and at work. They are the co-founders of "Lovetalks", a mission-driven kingdom expression focusing on purpose, marriage, and healthy relationships. They also lead the marriage ministry in their local church. They are passionate about supporting others in pursuing and discovering their purpose in God, building strong marriages and fostering healthy relationships. They believe marriage is the foundation of family life, and family is at the core of a thriving society.

They were involved in the Marriage Course run by Holy Trinity Anglican Church in Brompton, London (HTB) and are both members of the steering committee for Engage, a national network of Christian organisations that focuses on different areas of a relationship. They are also one of the presenters featured in "Marriage By Design", a pre-marriage DVD series developed by Care for the Family, and have encouraged, taught, counselled, and coached countless couples in building healthy marriages and homes.

Kemi and Bode speak on purpose, marriage and healthy relationships at conferences and seminars, sharing Godly insights and practical nuggets. They are also trained facilitators, behavioural consultants, and marriage counsellors.

www.ingramcontent.com/pod-product-compliance
Lightning Source LLC
LaVergne TN
LVHW051417080426
835508LV00022B/3128